The Salmon

This book has been reviewed
for accuracy by

Carroll R. Norden, Ph.D.
Professor of Zoology
University of Wisconsin—Milwaukee

Copyright © 1979, Raintree Publishers Limited

Library of Congress Number: 78-21178

1 2 3 4 5 6 7 8 9 0 83 82 81 80 79

Printed in the United States of America.

Library of Congress Cataloging in Publication Data

Hogan, Paula Z
  The salmon.

  Cover title: The life cycle of the salmon.
  SUMMARY: Presents a simple explanation of the life
cycle of a salmon.
  1. Salmon — Juvenile literature. [1. Salmon.
2. Fishes] I. Miyake, Yoshi. II.   Title. III. Title: The life cycle of the salmon.
QL638.S2H64   597'.55   78-21178
ISBN 0-8172-1255-8 lib. bdg.

The
SALMON

By Paula Z. Hogan
Illustrations by Yoshi Miyake

RAINTREE CHILDRENS BOOKS
Milwaukee • Toronto • Melbourne • London

4

The Salmon

Salmon eggs hatch in early
spring. The baby salmon are called
fry. They live in rivers.

After a few days, the fry swim
to the sea. The sea may be only a
few miles away. They swim at
night and hide during the day.

The fish go far from their home
river. Salmon eat small animals
that live in the sea.

Salmon are food for bigger fish.
In the dark, salmon are harder to
see. So they feed mostly at night.

After two years, pink salmon
are ready to lay eggs. They swim
back to their home river. They
know their home river by
its smell.

Along the way, the male salmon changes. His nose hooks. A hump grows on his back.

Many salmon never finish their trip home. They may be trapped in nets. Wild animals may catch them.

The fish stop eating when they
reach the river. Under the skin,
their meat turns red.

Some pink salmon lay eggs at
the mouth of the river. Others go
farther upstream.

First the female digs a nest. She turns on her side and pushes stones away with her tail. The male covers the eggs with sperm.

Then the female moves away to
lay more eggs. The male follows.
Stones wash over the nest.

Fully grown pink salmon never
go back to sea. After laying eggs,
they die.

The eggs stay in the nest all winter. Small stones hide the eggs from other animals. In spring, the eggs hatch. The fry swim to the sea.

Not all salmon are the same.
The dwarf salmon lives in lakes.
The chinook is the biggest salmon
of all. The Atlantic salmon does
not die after laying its eggs.

chinook salmon

Atlantic salmon

dwarf salmon

DATE DUE

DE 05 '85	NOV 21 '85		

DEMCO 38-297